STUDIO COMPANION SERIES

DESIGN BASICS

BOOK ONE

STUDIO COMPANION SERIES

STUDIO COMPANION SERIES

DESIGN BASICS

BOOK ONE

DONNA LYNNE FULLMER
IIDA, IDEC

KANSAS STATE UNIVERSITY
DEPARTMENT OF INTERIOR ARCHITECTURE
AND PRODUCT DESIGN

FAIRCHILD BOOKS
NEW YORK

Executive Director & General Manager: Michael Schluter

Executive Editor: Olga T. Kontzias

Assistant Acquisitions Editor: Amanda Breccia

Senior Development Editor: Joseph Miranda

Assistant Art Director: Sarah Silberg

Production Director: Ginger Hillman

Associate Production Editor: Linda Feldman

Project Editor: Jeff Hoffman

Copyeditor: Joanne Slike

Ancillaries Editor: Amy Butler

Associate Director of Sales: Melanie Sankel

Cover Design: Michael Miranda

Cover Art: Fergus MacNeill / Alamy

Text Design: Kendrek Lyons

Page Layout: Tom Helleberg

Library of Congress Catalog Card Number: 2011933638

ISBN: 978-1-60901-092-8

GST R 133004424

TP14

CONTENTS

||||||||||||||||||||||||||||||||||||||||||||||||||||||||||||||||||||||||||||||

PREFACE

The overall idea for this series of books came from the love of teaching the freshman design studio. What I have seen, time and time again, is a lack of basic design skills due to the influx of technology. While I believe in being a well-versed designer, I feel the computer is just another tool in the arsenal of what a student, and a professional, can bring to the table when it comes to designing. To this end, I feel hand skills, and the teaching of hand skills, has become a lost art.

I tell students that beginning the study of architecture and design is like starting kindergarten again, because we ask them to learn to write and draw in a new way. The books in the Studio Companion Series acknowledge that and act as an introduction to a skill through interactive lessons for each topic. I have seen firsthand how students increase their skills more rapidly by doing rather than just seeing. In addition, like it or not, today everyone wants things faster and easily digestible. I feel this format, with a lot of images and text that is direct and simple to read, will play to this audience of future designers.

The Studio Companion Series includes four books that address all the skill sets or topics discussed in beginning the study of architecture and design. Each book is compact and highly portable, and addresses each topic in a clear-cut and graphic manner. Each has been developed for today's students, who want information "down and dirty" and presented in an interactive way with simple examples on the topics. The series includes *Design Basics, Drafting Basics, 3D Design Basics,* and *Presentation Basics.*

Design Basics introduces students to the elements and principles of design, creating a vocabulary to discuss all forms of design. With its simple definitions and clear examples, *Design Basics* shows the student how to appreciate every type of design—even when it might not be his or her own personal taste. Armed with this design vocabulary, students can begin to create their own spaces. Exploring the design process can be a challenge, but the simple steps are outlined and examples given, making the navigation a bit easier.

This book is the result of years of teaching students all over the country and listening to their questions when they were using standard textbooks.

ACKNOWLEDGMENTS

The Studio Companion Series represents the result of working with students all over the country and the thrill I get watching the "lightbulbs go on" as they learn. There is nothing like seeing a student use a scale properly for the first time—it is an addiction to be a part of this type of learning. To all my students, thank you for giving me that charge and making me proud!

To my high school English teacher and to the men and women I work alongside every day, thank you for showing me how to listen to students and respond respectfully while maintaining the authority in the classroom.

Finally, everyone writes and says this, but I truly owe my career to my supportive and loving family, who have taught me things you could never find in a textbook.

STUDIO COMPANION SERIES

DESIGN
BASICS

BOOK ONE

ONE

ELEMENTS AND PRINCIPLES OF DESIGN

OBJECTIVES

You will be able to identify and analyze:

- The elements of design

- The principles of design

- The successful use of the elements and principles of design in interior and architectural settings

How do we look at something that another person has created and evaluate it, especially if we don't like it? Aesthetics, let's face it, are how we typically judge everything in our lives. Because all design is subjective, there need to be criteria on which to evaluate and judge, for example, a space, artwork, or clothing. The elements and principles of design allow us to do so while using a shared, objective terminology.

The elements of design are the components used to create an object, composition, or environment. They include the following:

- Point
- Line
- Shape + Plane
- Form + Mass
- Space + Volume
- Color
- Texture

The principles of design are the methods in which to organize the elements. They include the following:

- Balance
- Emphasis + Dominance
- Repetition + Rhythm
- Movement
- Proportion + Scale
- Unity + Harmony
- Variety

Once we have the definitions of these design terms, we can evaluate an interior space, building, painting, Web site, clothing collection, and so on by seeing how the designers used the elements and principles of design to create them. So even though we might not like the aesthetic of a particular item, we can have a better appreciation of it through understanding the elements and principles used.

In the following pages, each element and principle is first defined, and then followed by image examples.

THE ELEMENTS OF DESIGN

IIIIIIIIIIIIIIIIIIIIIIIIIIIIIIIIIIIIIIIIIIIIIIIIIIIIIIIIIIIIIIIIIIIIIIIIIIIIIIIIIIIIIIIIIIIIIIII

POINT

A point is a single position in a space or surface without length or width.

A series of points on two layered pieces of metal create a texture on the exterior of the building. (© *Jakob+MacFarlane. Photo by Nicolas Borel*)

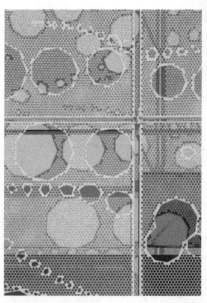

LINE

A line is a one-dimensional stroke that is greater in length than width.

Lines can provide graphic order. A horizontal line can bring a sense of calm and stability to people because they associate them with items in their everyday life, like the floor and horizon. A vertical line is more formal and usually provides visual balance; think, for instance, of a row of columns on the outside of a bank or post office. Lines also provide movement and can be straight, angled, curved, wavy, and organic.

Lines have the properties of length, direction, and position. They can be thick or thin, segmented, dashed, or dotted.

Horizontal and vertical lines are used to order the space and bring the eye up. (© Jakob+MacFarlane. Photo by Nicolas Borel)

Lines are seen on both the walls and ceiling, creating rhythm and order in the space. (*Ezra Stoller © Esto*)

Geometric and organic lines are used to take the viewer through the space with whimsy and energy. (© *ARTonFILE.com*)

Diagonal lines pull the viewer's eye up the staircase, while the regulating lines created by the stairs rhythmically march us into the space. (© *Ralph Lieberman*)

A variety of horizontal lines are used to create pattern and texture. Some lines are dashed to create movement across the building. (© *ARTonFILE.com*)

SHAPE + PLANE

A plane is a closed line that creates a shape. It is two-dimensional and expresses length and width with hardly any depth.

Shapes can be geometric, like circles, triangles, rectangles, and squares, or they can be free formed and organic, like amoebas.

Specific shapes have certain meanings. A circle typically indicates unity; a triangle, stability. Whereas a square has a more formal quality.

Shapes have the properties of orientation and position within a composition or space.

Planes and shapes are created by the mullions in the glass as well as the glass panes themselves. Repetition of these planes is seen across the entire façade of the building. (© *ARTonFILE.com*)

Planes are used to create the walls, floors, ceilings, and pool in this pavilion. Planes can be made solid as with the granite slabs, translucent in the glass, or even natural with the small wading pool. (*Mies van der Rohe Ludwig [1886–1969] © ARS,NY; German pavillion for the International Art Exhibit, Barcelona, 1929. Location: Exhibition Pavillion, Barcelona, Spain. Photo credit: Erich Lessing / Art Resource, NY*)

The chair is composed of planes and lines that float together to create a structure similar to a multistory building. (*Gerrit Thomas Rietveld [Dutch, 1888–1964] Berlin Chair [reproduction], designed 1923, reproduced 1981, Lacquer, 41 3/4 x 29 1/8 x 22 9/16 in. [106.05 x 73.98 x 57.31 cm], Milwaukee Art Museum, Layton Art Collection, Purchase L1982.160. Photo credit: John R. Glembin © 2011 Artists Rights Society [ARS], New York*)

FORM + MASS

Forms are shapes with dimension. They express length, width, and depth.

A form is three dimensional and can include points, lines, and planes. Spheres, pyramids, cylinders, cones, and boxes are all forms.

Forms have the properties of surface, orientation, and position.

The six major rectangular forms create the entire building. Each has its own unique shape, but expressed together, they give the building its own mass. (*Courtesy of Jeffrey E. Klee, Colonial Williamsburg Foundation*)

This building campus demonstrates a variety of forms and volumes. The pool form reaches out to pull the viewer into the space. The building on the left is made up of repeating balcony masses defining a rectangle. The building in the background uses undulating rectangular forms to create a curved front façade. (© *ARTonFILE.com*)

The organic, curvilinear form of this sculpture is playful against the hard lines and angles of the building behind it. (© ARTonFILE.com)

This building demonstrates planes and masses. The vertical members of the structure are highly textured with small masses of stone, while the cantilevered patios are smooth and large forms. (*Ezra Stoller © Esto*)

SPACE + VOLUME

Space is the area defined by elements being around one another, whether on top or below such as a ceiling or floor, or in front or behind such as a wall or series of columns. It is the three-dimensional volume enclosed within planes and forms—literally, such as furniture in a room, or figuratively, such as in a painting of a street. Space creates depth in two-dimensional art.

Space has layers: a background, a middle ground, and a foreground. The background indicates depth, the middle ground can include the horizon line, and the foreground is what is the closest to the viewer.

In addition to layers, space can be positive or negative. Positive space is the area taken up by an item or subject, whereas the space remaining around it is negative space.

Repeated forms are used in different materials to create the overall volume of this home. Two opposing solid-looking forms balance the home, while the glass forms create light and openness in the structure. (*Ezra Stoller © Esto*)

Literally, this corrugated metal and concrete tube creates a space for a train to enter this building. Space is also created underneath the tracks to emphasize the pedestrian entrance to the building. (© *ARTonFILE.com*)

This structure is delicate and hints at the linear structure behind the translucent panels. However, the reflection off of the glossy panels indicates the massive space seen in the landscape. (© *ARTonFILE.com*)

Space is well defined and captured within this image. The perforated ceiling and walls allow the viewer to glimpse the structure and building support systems. The foreground indicates a lot of texture and defined space around each jagged stone and wispy plant. The large indentations in the wall almost entice the observer to go into them. (© *ARTonFILE.com*)

The light and layering of lines and textures create space within the cavelike structure. (© *speirce/www.canyonlights.com*)

COLOR

The amount of information available on color and color theory is extraordinary and should be explored for a more comprehensive understanding. For the purpose of this book, we will just look at the basics.

Color, literally, is the light reflected off an object. It has three major characteristics. The first is the hue, or the name of the color itself—red, yellow, or blue. How light or dark a color is or the range of a color is referred to as the value. Finally, the intensity of a color refers to its brightness or dullness. Color will be further explored in Chapter 2.

The exterior of this building uses values and intensities of several hues beautifully. (*Scagliola / Brakkee / © Neutelings Riedijk Architecten*)

The large tile backsplash in this restroom uses many hues and overlaps them to create additional colors and values. (*© Prizeotel Management Group*)

TEXTURE

Texture is the surface quality of an item that can be seen or felt. That surface can be rough or smooth, soft or hard, cold or hot.

Textures are defined as being tactile—that is, how something actually feels—or visual, how something looks like it would feel. For example, a drawing of a cactus may look like it has sharp and dangerous needles, but when you touch the drawing, the paper is smooth.

Sleek and etched patterned metal against a rough roof plane shows the extremes of textures in one building. (© ARTonFILE.com)

Metal louvers create repetition and a smooth texture against the rough, stamped concrete panel. (© *ARTonFILE.com*)

A patchwork texture is created with metal panels on an organically shaped, bulbous building. (© *Hartill Art Associates, London, Canada*)

This elaborate façade
uses intricate and traditional
carved statues in combination
with a series of organic free
forms for unique textures.
(© ARTonFILE.com)

The material contradiction of the smooth concrete
flooring and high-gloss light fixtures with the rough
texture of the stone and wood walls and ceiling
shows the extremes textures can play in a design.
(*Photo by Seven Ascona*)

PRINCIPLES
OF DESIGN

||||||||||||||||||||||||||||||||||||||||||||||||||||||||||||||||||||||||||||||||||||||||||||||

Principles of design are the methods by which elements are organized. Several can be used at a time, and they often complement each other in a finished piece or space.

BALANCE

Balance is the visual weight of the elements within a space or composition. There are three types of balance: symmetrical, asymmetrical, and radial. In symmetrical balance, the elements used on one side of the design are very similar to those on the other side visually. Asymmetrical balance, on the other hand, has dissimilar items on both sides, but they may still look balanced in weight. Finally, in radial balance, the elements are arranged around a center point, like the spokes of a wheel. These elements may or may not be similar.

Symmetrical balance is evident along the center aisle with the chairs, altar rails, and architecture of the ceiling and walls. (*Courtesy of Whit Slemmons*)

The pews, strong angular architecture, and repeating light fixtures create symmetrical balance in this house of worship. (© *Hartill Art Associates, London, Canada*)

At an initial look, this Spanish colonial church appears to be symmetrical. However, upon closer evaluation, the walls of the church are asymmetrical with the exterior windows and pulpit. (© *speirce / www.canyonlights.com*)

Radial balance begins with a center rosette and wood trim and expands to include archways and stained glass windows. (© *Hartill Art Associates, London, Canada*)

EMPHASIS + DOMINANCE

Emphasis, or the focal point, is the item that catches the viewer's attention or dominates the design. A designer or artist can make a component the emphasis through contrast, scale, color, texture, and shape.

Emphasis is demonstrated in the balance of the benches but specifically in the light creating the cross on the rear wall. (© Renee Burri / Magnum Photos)

The altar and nave are celebrated as the emphasis in the space through balanced symmetry and as a focal point under the domed space. (© *Hartill Art Associates, London, Canada*)

The space and volume above the two cantilevered balconies creates emphasis within this museum. (© ARTonFILE.com)

A series of arched windows, elaborate trim, and stained glass creates the dominance of this dome in this church. (© Hartill Art Associates, London, Canada)

REPETITION + RHYTHM

Repetition is simple; elements are repeated throughout a design. A series of evenly spaced columns down a hallway is a good example of repetition. It can help to create unity and stability.

Rhythm, which is similar, is the repetition of one or more elements, not necessarily evenly spaced but in an organized manner. Rhythm can create movement and give the viewer a sense of elements bouncing or dancing around a piece or space. Rhythm can also create a pattern.

A classical Greek temple is the epitome of a repetition of columns. (© *speirce / www. canyonlights.com*)

The grass stepping stones create a rhythm to jump upon as you approach the building. The texture of the façade also illustrates repetition of the organic forms on each panel. (© *ARTonFILE.com*)

The screens seem to be dancing down upon the altar, creating a unique, light rhythm. (*Ezra Stoller © Esto*)

Repetition of horizontal lines is clearly seen in the adjustable window screens and corrugated ceiling materials. It is also seen in the repetitive forms of the light fixtures in the study carrels. Finally, a vertical repetition is seen in the candlestick columns. (*© ARTonFILE.com*)

MOVEMENT

Movement is the path taken through artwork or space, which often leads to the focal point. It can be directed along lines, shapes, or colors.

The roof structure reaches up and over the concert hall to create a wave of music crashing into the building. (© Richard Bryant / Arcaid / Corbis)

This shade structure feels as if the fingers could dance in the wind. (Calatrava, Santiago [b. 1951] © Copyright. Installation view of the exhibition, "Santiago Calatrava: Structure and Expression." March 25, 1993, through May 18, 1993. The Museum of Modern Art, New York. Photographic Archive. The Museum of Modern Art Archives, New York. Photo: Mali Olatunji. The Museum of Modern Art, New York, NY, USA. Digital Image © The Museum of Modern Art / Licensed by SCALA Art Resource, NY)

The rods supporting the staircase create tense movement up stepping-stone spiral stair treads. (*Ezra Stoller © Esto*)

The fluid concrete forms flow across the lines of the entire building façade. (*Ezra Stoller © Esto*)

PROPORTION + SCALE

Proportion is when all the parts of the whole visually relate well with one another. It creates a sense of unity and balance.

There are many types and theories of proportion as well as proportioning systems. Some of the most common are the Fibonacci series also referred to as the "golden section," and the famous architect Le Corbusier's Modulor.

The Fibonacci series is the infinite sequence of numbers that is derived by adding a number to its previous number to arrive at the next number (e.g., 1, 2, 3, 5, 8, 13 …). The golden section, often denoted by the Greek letter Φ (phi), is, roughly, the ratio of a number in the Fibonacci series to its previous number (3:2, 5:3, etc.). Both result in a pleasing relationship of items to one another in a space or piece of art. The golden section can be found not only in things made by human beings but also in nature.

(opposite page) The growth of each segment of this Romanesco Broccoli/Cauliflower has the spiral of the golden section. (© *Antonio M. Rosario/ Tetra Images/Corbis*)

An overlay of the golden section on the Parthenon indicates the proportional relationship between the columns, cornice, and frieze. (© *Fergus McNeill/Alamy*)

Le Corbusier's Modulor is an example of anthropometric scale that looks at the size and proportion of man to himself, to others, and to his environment.

An original drawing of Le Corbusier's Modulor indicates proportion as it is relative to man. (*Le Corbusier [Charles-Edouard Jeanneret, 1887–1965] © ARS, NY. "D." Location: Private collection. Photo credit: Erich Lessing/Art Resource, NY*)

This leads nicely to the principle of scale. There are two types of scale: human and visual scale.

Human scale is the relationship we have to a space. Americans are used to a 6 ft., 8 in. door, so when one is shorter or taller, we notice it right away because it is out of the "normal" human scale.

Visual scale is the relationship of the parts to the whole or proportion.

The large volume of this art museum is more understandable by placing a person in the space to see the relativity of the space to human beings. (© ARTonFILE.com)

Frank Lloyd Wright famously compresses people in his building entrances only to open up the space to make it feel larger. (*Ezra Stoller © Esto*)

UNITY + HARMONY

Unity is an agreement between all parts of a space, creating a sense of harmony. As it pertains to design, harmony is often associated with Gestalt psychology or theory, which states that "the whole is more than the sum of its parts." This means that the entire space or painting is unified and we get the sense it all belongs together. A great deal has been written on Gestalt psychology and can be further explored for a deeper understanding.

Unity is seen through color first and then shapes in this ceiling. (*Jonathan M. Bloom and Sheila S. Blair*)

The depth of this doorway demonstrates unity through materials but variety through texture. The texture does not detract from the doorway, which exemplifies the idea of unity. (© *Hartill Art Associates, London, Canada*)

The repetition of balcony forms creates unity on the façade, but the colored transparent handrails create visual interest. (© *ARTonFILE.com*)

Harmony is first evident through the repetition of exterior wall planes and columns; the glass wreaths also unify the space while providing variety through color. (*Pacific Lutheran University*)

VARIETY

Variety uses several elements of design to hold the attention of the viewer. It can guide the eye through the artwork or space.

Keep in mind that variety can become overwhelming and should be used carefully.

Variety can simply be the integration of two or three styles of architecture in one space.
(© *Hartill Art Associates, London, Canada*)

Curved lines, straight lines, and bent geometric forms demonstrate variety in this exterior façade.
(© *ARTonFILE.com*)

This space demonstrates variety by integrating curvilinear solid forms with geometric transparent planes. (*Ezra Stoller © Esto*)

SUMMARY

||||||||||||||||||||||||||||||||||||||||||||||||||||||||||||||||||||||||||||||||||||||||||||

Understanding the elements and principles of design allows us to gain insight into a designer's thought process, and although we might not care for the end result, we can have an appreciation for the final design.

EXERCISES

||||||||||||||||||||||||||||||||||||||||||||||||||||||||||||||||||||||||||||||||||||||||||||||||||||

IDENTIFICATION

Practice identifying the elements and principles of design using the following steps and photographs:

1. Place a piece of tracing paper over the image.
2. Draw registration marks in all four corners of the image on the tracing paper so you can maintain your place.
3. Trace one element or principle of design and label it on the sheet.
4. Remove that sheet and place another one over the photograph and repeat the process.

Once you have a series of tracing papers, layer them on one another without the original photograph underneath. You should start to see the re-creation of the original image through the tracing paper layers, confirming the successful use of the elements and principles of design in the space.

Radial balance is first seen surrounding the center tile. Repetition is seen in the surrounding tiles through tile shapes and colors. (*Photo by Walter B. Denny*)

Place tracing paper over the image and add registration marks.

Radial balance is traced over the image.

Repetition of shape is traced over the image.

The exterior of this building demonstrates repetition of horizontal and vertical lines and rhythm of rectangular forms in the stepping stones. (*Dov Friedman*)

Repetition of lines is evident in the details surrounding the two windows of this building. (© *ARTonFILE.com*)

Symmetrical balance is seen about the aisle with the altar,
benches, and stained glass windows. Repetition of form
is seen in the cylindrical light fixtures. (*Jerry Anderson*)

Harmony
and unity are
seen in the
colored and
rectangular
planes on the
exterior of
the building.
(© ARTonFILE
.com)

The curved lines and archways repeat down the corridor, which is a seductive curve that intrigues the viewer into following it around to see the space promised on the other side. (© *Hartill Art Associates, London, Canada*)

EVALUATION

As you see successful spaces, in life or in books and magazines, take a photograph or copy the images and evaluate which elements and principles are being used. This allows you to see patterns or consistencies in the work you like and can influence how you design in the future.

TWO

COLOR
THEORY

OBJECTIVES

You will be able to identify and understand:

- The vocabulary of color
- Color schemes
- The effects of specific colors

COLOR IS AN AMAZING ELEMENT OF DESIGN. IT CAN AFFECT THE VIEWER'S PERCEPTION OF EVERYTHING IN AN INTERIOR SPACE OR IN A PIECE OF ARTWORK, AS WELL AS HOW ELEMENTS IN A SPACE RELATE TO ONE ANOTHER. COLOR HAS PERSONAL, CULTURAL, AND GLOBAL CONNOTATIONS AND SHOULD NOT BE TAKEN LIGHTLY IN DESIGN.

THIS CHAPTER IS MEANT TO BE A CONDENSED LOOK AT THE VOCABULARY OF COLOR, BASIC COLOR SCHEMES, AND THE EFFECTS COLOR CAN HAVE. IT IS JUST A QUICK OVERVIEW OF AN INFINITELY VAST SUBJECT.

VOCABULARY

||||||||||||||||||||||||||||||||||||||||||||||||||||||||||||||||||||||||||||||||||||||||||||||||||

As discussed in the previous chapter, color, literally, is the light reflected off an object. It has three major characteristics.

The first is the *hue* or the name of the color itself—red, yellow, blue, and so on. A hue can generate several colors. Raspberry, poppy, maroon, and carmine are all colors; but the hue is red.

Value refers to the lightness or darkness of a hue that is being altered by adding white or black to the color. Adding white lightens the hue and produces a *tint*. Adding black darkens the hue and produces a *shade*.

The *intensity* or saturation of a color refers to the brightness or dullness of the color when compared to gray.

COLOR WHEEL

||||||||||||||||||||||||||||||||||||||||||||||||||||||||||||||||||||||||||||||||||||||||||||||||||||||||||||||

Sir Isaac Newton put white light through a glass prism and it fractured the light into multiple colors. In essence, he created the first color wheel by discovering the circular attributes of the color spectrum. Although there have been dozens of color wheels developed over several centuries, designers today generally use the Prang, or artist's color wheel, developed by Louis Prang.

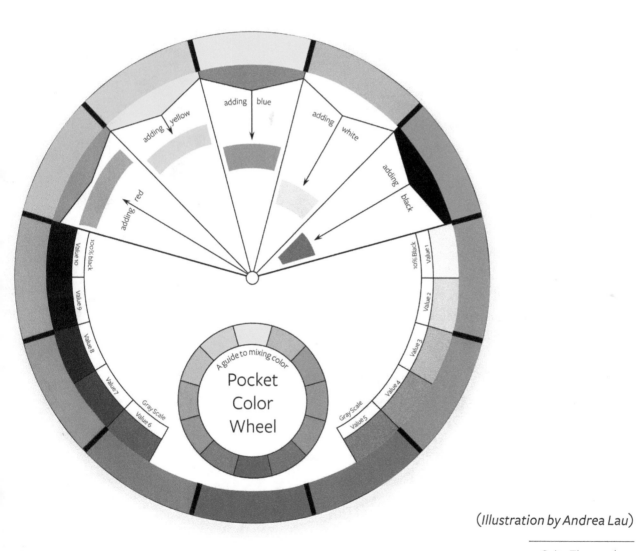

(Illustration by Andrea Lau)

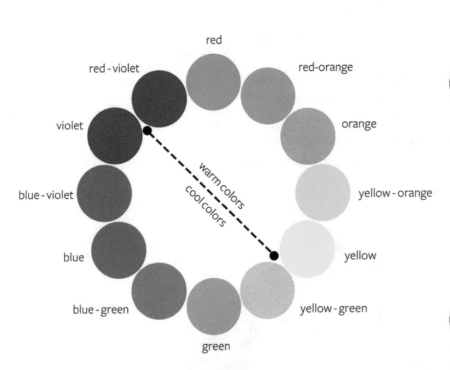

red

red-violet

red-orange

violet

orange

warm colors
cool colors

blue-violet

yellow-orange

blue

yellow

blue-green

yellow-green

green

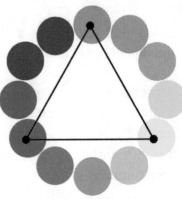

Primary Colors

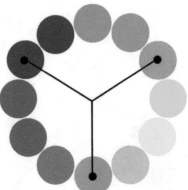

Secondary Colors

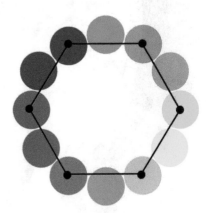

Tertiary Colors

The typical color wheel has 12 standard colors.

The *primary colors,* red, yellow, and blue, cannot be made from the other colors within the color wheel; however, mixing them together creates the remaining nine.

Secondary colors are crafted by mixing two primary colors together, which results in orange, green, and violet (purple).

One primary color and one adjacent secondary color mixed together create a *tertiary* or *intermediate color* resulting in red-orange, yellow-orange, yellow-green, blue-green, blue-violet, or red-violet.

Most color wheels allow you to rotate a window to reveal a new color that will be created when combining any two colors on the wheel and by adding white or black to the original color.

On the back of the color wheel you will find the color relationships. First are the tint, tone, and shade of each of the 12 colors. The color schemes are indicated graphically in the center of the wheel and expose the colors in each scheme through small windows. Rotating the wheel allows you to see all the options.

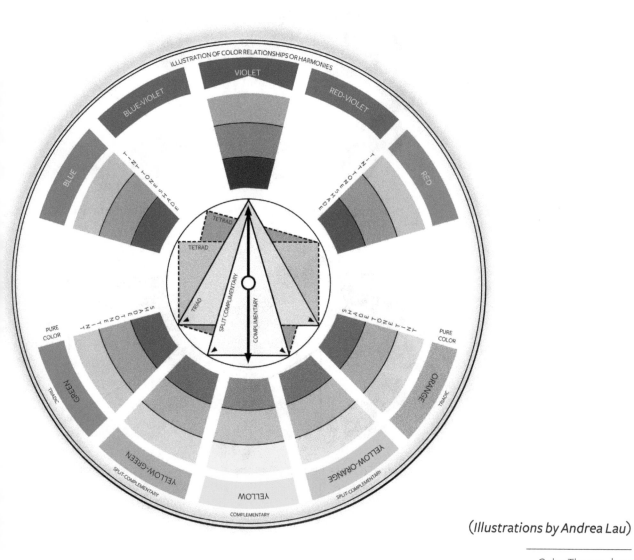

(Illustrations by Andrea Lau)

COLOR SCHEMES

|||||||||||||||||||||||||||||||||||||||||||||||||||||||||||||||||||||||||||||||||||||||||||||||||||

A color scheme is a predetermined group of colors or hues—with one exception, the monochromatic scheme—which work well with one another.

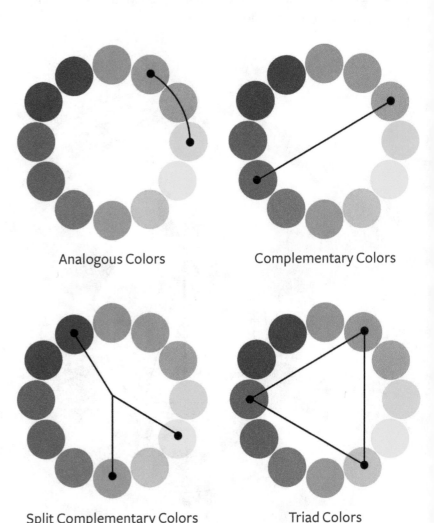

Analogous Colors

Complementary Colors

Split Complementary Colors

Triad Colors

(Illustration by Andrea Lau)

A *monochromatic* color scheme is a range of tints, shades, and tones of one single color.

An *analogous* color scheme is similar to a monochromatic scheme, except it uses tints, shades, and tones of colors that are adjacent on the color wheel.

Red tints, shades, and tones create a monochromatic color scheme as seen in the upholstery, carpet, lighting, and even the wood veneered walls. (© *Andrea Martiradonna*)

An analogous color scheme of red, orange, yellow-orange, and yellow is used in this contemporary kitchen design. (*iStockphoto* / © *poligonchik*)

Drama and light are evident in this complementary color scheme of red and green. The use of soft red fabric in relationship to the hard glowing green walls makes the space feel evocative. (*Starck Network*)

Complementary colors are directly opposite on the color wheel. All the tints, shades, and tones of those colors can be used in this color scheme.

Split complementary colors create a thin triangle on the color wheel. You begin with the complementary colors but take the two adjacent colors to one of the complementary colors to complete the triangle. So, red, yellow-green, and blue-green make a split complementary color scheme.

An unusual split complementary color scheme creates lively and dynamic spaces within a hotel. Each individual area is unified through the use of this color scheme, even in the small linen detail in the guest room. (© *Prizeotel Management Group*)

A color scheme typically reserved for children's design is simplified but sophisticated in this hallway. The yellow is infused with the sunlight, while the red calls attention to the end of the hall, where the blue creates a restful destination. (© *2011 Artists Rights Society [ARS], New York / Pro Litteris, Zurich*)

A *triad* color scheme creates an equilateral triangle on the color wheel. For example, the three primary colors make a triad color scheme. The three secondary colors create another.

Tetrad color schemes can be difficult to contain due to the use of four hues. This small restaurant uses a tetrad of yellow-green, blue-green, red-orange, and red-violet as upholstery fabric and a light surface glow successfully. (*Courtesy of Karim Rashid Inc.*)

A *tetrad* color scheme creates a rectangle or square on the color wheel.

EFFECTS
OF COLOR

||||||||||||||||||||||||||||||||||||||||||||||||||||||||||||||||||||||||||||||||||||||||||||||||||

WARM AND COOL COLORS

Warm colors are red, orange, and yellow, which remind people of the desert, fire, or the sun. Typically they tend to advance or move forward in a composition or space.

Cool colors are blue, purple, and green, which people associate with water, ice, and grass. Cool colors tend to recede into a composition or space.

Red is exciting, sensual, and aggressive. It has been proven that red can raise someone's blood pressure, so keep this in mind when using it. Red is seen in the fast-food industry to encourage people not to stay too long and to eat quickly. Red should not be used in jails or prisons and should be used selectively in schools, as it stimulates activity.

(*LivedIn Images* / © *Nathan Willock* / *VIEW*)

(*iStockphoto* / © *Arpad Benedek*)

Orange is cheerful and bold. It has been shown to decrease hostility and irritability. Orange has very little negative association, so it is an acceptable color to use when designing for diverse cultures.

Yellow is associated with sunshine and warmth. It is highly visible and is often used for safety purposes. It is a challenging color to use successfully in interior design and fashion, as it reacts differently with various skin tones.

(*iStockphoto / © Holger Mette*)

(*LivedIn Images* / © *Marc Gerritsen*)

Green is a restful, calm color and reminds people of growth and nature. It can read as a neutral color and is often used in health-care and educational facilities.

Blue is the most preferred color by Americans. It reminds people of the sea and sky, stability and loyalty, authority and peace. It is the most flattering color on the most people.

(iStockphoto / © Mlenny Photography)

(*LivedIn Images* / © *Hufton + Crow* / *VIEW*)

Purple is a royal and elegant color. It has been shown to lower blood pressure and promote creativity. Too much purple can overwhelm, so it should be used sparingly. Also, because it is a blend of red and blue, two hues that have very different effects on people, the particular color of purple should be chosen carefully.

SUMMARY

||||||||||||||||||||||||||||||||||||||||||||||||||||||||||||||||||||||||||||||||||||||||||||

The impact and use of color is a powerful and consistently influencing element in design. Thoughtful and strategic care should be used when you are selecting colors for a building or space.

THREE

THE DESIGN PROCESS

OBJECTIVES

You will be able to identify and understand:

- The phases in the design process
- The potential tasks associated with each phase
- The potential deliverables with each phase

THERE IS A METHOD TO THE MADNESS OF DESIGN. IT IS CALLED THE DESIGN PROCESS, AND IT HAS SIX BASIC STEPS. THESE STEPS ARE SIMILAR IN ANY DESIGN EFFORT, FROM WEB SITE DESIGN TO FASHION DESIGN, AND THE DESIGNER WILL GO THROUGH THESE STEPS TO COMPLETE A PROJECT.

1. PROGRAMMING
2. SCHEMATIC DESIGN (SD)
3. DESIGN DEVELOPMENT (DD)
4. CONSTRUCTION DOCUMENTATION (CD)
5. CONSTRUCTION ADMINISTRATION (CA)
6. POSTOCCUPANCY EVALUATION (POE)

Each step has a series of tasks that occur and a series of end products. The design team does these tasks with consultants and the client.

The design team is typically composed of individuals who represent three major categories:

- Design: Members are responsible for the design or "look" of the project.

- Management: Members are responsible for client relations, the design team, and the financial issues relating to the project.

- Technical: Members are responsible for the documentation and overseeing the building of the project.

Each assumes a specific role that is integral to the success of a job and will participate as needed in the design process.

Consultant involvement can vary from job to job but can include the following:

- Engineers: Types of engineers include mechanical, electrical, plumbing, structural, and acoustical, to name a few. Each member from these groups will participate in the design process in similar ways to the design team: designing, managing, or overseeing the technical information.

- Specialty design: Examples include lighting designers, kitchen designer for restaurants, security system designers, and graphic designer for signage packages. As with the consultants, they will participate as needed in the process.

Some firms require signatures, or sign-offs, from the client, ensuring that a step is complete before moving on to the next.

The tasks and end products, or "deliverables," as they are referred to, are outlined for everyone participating in the contract and can include documents, models, presentations, and drawings. Deviation from the outline can result in changes to every aspect of the project, including the time frame, financial issues, and the project's overall success.

It is important to know all the steps in the design process; however, you typically will go only through the first three steps in your first year of study. As you move forward in your studies, you will learn more about the final three steps. To this end, examples of student work will be shown only for the first three steps, at the end of the chapter, while images of Frank Gehry's design solution for the Guggenheim Museum in Bilbao, Spain, will be included with each phase. The final built museum is seen here as a reference, as you see each phase of the design process unfold.

Exterior view of the completed museum.
(© *Dennis Stock / Magnum Photos*)

Interior view of the completed museum. (*Photograph courtesy of the Visual Resources Collection, School of Architecture, The University of Texas at Austin*)

  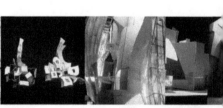

PROGRAMMING

||||||||||||||||||||||||||||||||||||||||||||||||||||||||||||||||||||||||||||||||||||||||||||||||||||||||||||||||||||||||||||||

The first step in the design process is called *programming*. The programming phase involves a lot of discussion, research, and gathering of information. This is when you get to know the clients, their needs, their existing situations, their future goals—basically the who, what, where, when, and why of their daily routines. This is true of both residential and commercial clients.

Some tasks that might occur during this phase include the following:

- Interviews with the client
- Completing questionnaires that the design firm has developed by project type including restaurants, law firms, retail, and so on
- Visits to the new site (referred to as site visits) to document existing conditions and architectural constraints
- Inventory of the client's existing furniture, fixtures, and equipment (referred to as FF&E)
- Analysis of existing space (square footage needs, adjacency requirements, etc.)
- Evaluation of other potential locations for the client
- Case studies of similar projects
- Research of current issues and trends for the client's industry

The deliverable at the end of the programming phase is a detailed report called a program. It may include the following:

- Text
  - Summary of the project size and location
  - Summary statement regarding the look and feel for the project, referred to as a concept statement
  - Key project goals that were identified
- Spreadsheets or charts
  - Quantity of employees by title and department
  - Square footage recommendations for employees and areas needed
  - Adjacency requirements for the planning of the space
  - Furniture requirements
  - Meeting room analysis
- Drawings
  - Prototypical drawings for offices, meeting rooms, and so on
  - Rough floor plans with areas called out by square footage, for a variety of potential locations. This can be referred to as a test fit analysis. It is done to see which building might be better suited for the client and can result in substantial savings in construction and/or a lease agreement
  - Big-idea drawings for the look of the space, otherwise known as concept sketches
  - Initial site evaluations, which could include evaluation of views or wind directions on the site
  - Drawings for proposed layouts called *adjacency* or *bubble diagrams,* which show how areas of the floor plan might relate to one another

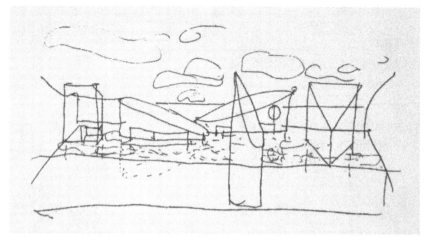

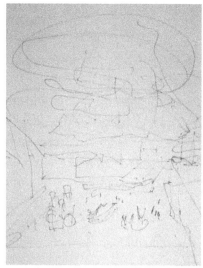

A concept or massing sketch by Frank Gehry. Quick sketches allow for ideas to come out of your thoughts and onto paper. Many are not evident in the final design solution, but their use is necessary in the design process. (*Photograph courtesy of the Visual Resources Collection, School of Architecture, The University of Texas at Austin*)

Concept sketch by Frank Gehry for Guggenheim Museum. A lot of professional architects have loose sketching styles; however, if the sketch speaks to them and provides a springboard for design development, that is all that matters. (*Photograph courtesy of the Visual Resources Collection, School of Architecture, The University of Texas at Austin*)

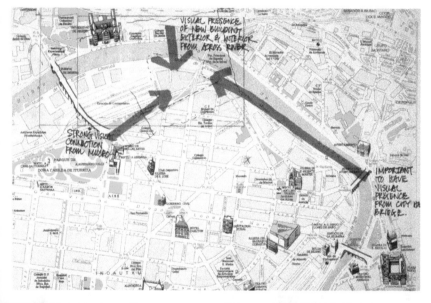

Initial site evaluation for the Guggenheim Museum in Bilbao, Spain. An understanding of the site is critical for both interior and exterior design success. (*Photograph courtesy of the Visual Resources Collection, School of Architecture, The University of Texas at Austin*)

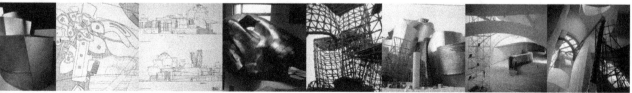

Another approach to programming can be read in an excellent, in-depth book titled *Problem Seeking: An Architectural Programming Primer* by William M. Peña and Steven A. Parshall (4th ed., New York, NY: John Wiley, 2001). These authors approach the programming phase by looking at five steps with four constraints. The five steps include the following:

- Establish *goals*.
- Collect and analyze *facts*.
- Uncover and test *concepts*.
- Determine *needs*.
- State the *problem*.

The authors look at these steps while keeping four constraints in mind. They are *function, form, economy,* and *time.*

As an example:

- A law firm *needs* a meeting space for the five partners and a secretary.

- The *function* is a meeting with a table and a minimum of six chairs.

- This can be handled in an enclosed room for privacy, which is a *goal* for any discussion within a law firm.

- A room needed to handle this type of meeting should take the *form* of at least 12 ft. x 12 ft.

- After evaluating the other meeting needs of the firm, resulting from the interviews and questionnaires, it is determined that several other groups within the firm could use a room that seats six people. Because the partner meeting occurs only once a month, it is more economical, and a better use of *time*, for this room to be used by the entire firm.

Regardless of the method of determining all that the client needs, the programming phase is crucial for a successful project. The report, charts, and drawings done in this phase will be used for the next step for the project. Their accuracy and thoroughness is essential.

SCHEMATIC DESIGN

The schematic design (SD) phase is when all the options are explored. Within this phase, discussions are still happening with the client, and a series of meetings could be set to review information. Preliminary coordination will also take place with any consultants, including engineers. Some tasks and deliverables that might occur during this phase include the following:

- Several floor plan layouts, known as space plans, that adhere to the program document requirements.
- Quick and simple rip and tear models of spaces to see if big ideas are working before committing them to the design.
- Layouts for furniture, mechanical, plumbing, electrical, and lighting plans.
- Initial selections for furniture, fixtures, and equipment (FF&E). For example, at this stage of the design, for a meeting room chair, you might be considering a chair with casters or a sled-base chair with bent metal legs or a four-legged chair.
- Concept and idea boards composed of images and inspirational items that can influence, and help a client understand, the design.
- Options for materials and finishes in the space. Should you use carpet or tile? Which is better suited for which space? Further exploration would then include the type, color, and size for each tile or carpet.
- Coordination with engineers.
- Local codes and disability issues. Disability issues include considerations of the Americans with Disabilities Act, commonly referred to as the ADA.
- Preliminary design sketches, typically hand drawn, of big ideas or detailed areas of the design.
- Entering basic project information into the computer, including dimensions of the outer shell of the building and drawings that will be shared with consultants. This step can include the drawing set up by establishing sheet sizes, naming conventions/guidelines, and so on.
- Determining preliminary construction budget.

The space-planning process must address the program developed earlier. Using an overall plan of the space, you should begin to graphically document the items listed below. Typically this is done using several pieces of tracing paper on top of the original plan.

- Existing conditions
  - Entrance and exit locations
  - Architectural constraints
    - Exterior walls
    - Structural walls or columns
    - Existing mechanical, plumbing, and electrical
  - Where are the best views?
  - What surrounds the space or building?
  - How was the space constructed?
- Design issues
  - Space allocations from the programming document
  - Floor plans with adjacencies and layouts
    - Developed from the initial bubble diagrams to create block plans first. A block plan indicates the size and shape of a space and its relationship to all the other spaces.
      - This step may have been completed in the programming phase as part of the test fit process in determining into which building the client will best fit.
  - Required square footages

Some deliverables that might occur prior to beginning the next design phase include the following:

- Finalized space plan at about 85 percent. There may be some minor issues that require more specific research prior to finalizing the layout. This could be due to specialized areas or equipment, missing information from the client, and so on.

- Refined layouts for furniture, mechanical, plumbing, electrical, and lighting plans.

- Study models. These models would be more refined than the initial rip and tear models, being created to scale and potentially with materials and finishes indicated.

- Refined FF&E selections with samples. At this point, you may know that you will be using a task chair with casters and an adjustable back but have not narrowed in on the specific manufacturer or fabric selections.

- Refined materials and finishes selections with samples. As with the FF&E, these selections may have been narrowed down from all the flooring options to carpet, for example.

- Hard-line, hand-drawn, or computer-generated sketches to communicate the overall or specific design ideas. These drawings can be colored, or rendered as we say in the industry, to more accurately represent the design solutions.

At the conclusion of this phase, a client should have approved all the items presented and be ready to refine the design down to every last detail. With this phase of exploration complete and solid selections made, you are ready for the third step in the design process.

Rough rip and tear models allow for quick design exploration without a lot of commitment; however, the exercise is invaluable, as seen in this series of models. (*Photograph courtesy of the Visual Resources Collection, School of Architecture, The University of Texas at Austin*)

Interior rip and tear models allow an understanding of elements and principles of form, mass, and scale. (*Photograph courtesy of the Visual Resources Collection, School of Architecture, The University of Texas at Austin*)

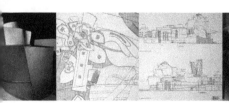

DESIGN DEVELOPMENT

The design development (DD) phase is all about refinement. All the choices made in the previous schematic design phase will be made more specific. Details will be determined for every aspect of the project.

Some tasks and deliverables that might occur during this phase include the following:

- Revisions to the space plan

- Revisions to the furniture, mechanical, plumbing, electrical, and lighting plans

- Revised design intent drawings from the sketches presented in the previous phase

- Commencement of interior architectural detailing, which can include custom millwork

- Detailed options given for materials and finishes as well as FF&E

- Refined design sketches, which may or may not be drawn with the use of the computer, of big ideas or detailed areas of the design

- Coordination with engineers

- Codes and ADA reviews

- Commencement of preliminary construction documentation, which is the next phase of the design process

- Refinement and updating of budgets

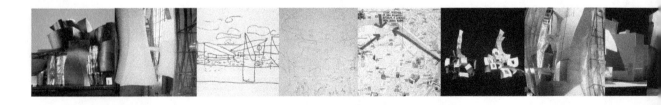

Some deliverables that might occur prior to beginning the next design phase include the following:

- Finalized floor plan

- Finalized furniture, mechanical, plumbing, electrical, and lighting plans

- Finalized design intent drawings

- Selected and approved materials and finishes as well as FF&E

- Final codes and ADA review

- Refinement and updating of budgets

This phase is complete when every aspect of the design has been approved and is ready to be built. To build a project, the design firm and consultants must prepare construction documents, which happens in the fourth step of the design process. These documents include the construction drawings and a written specification book.

Final exterior study model. The final design is understood with material selections, signage, interior to exterior relationships, and the sense of human scale. (*Photograph courtesy of the Visual Resources Collection, School of Architecture, The University of Texas at Austin*)

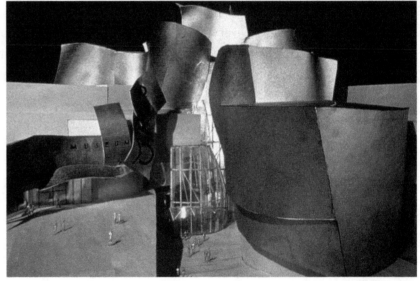

Interior atrium study model. Final models not only address the overall form of the space but indicate materials, scale, and proportion. (*Photograph courtesy of the Visual Resources Collection, School of Architecture, The University of Texas at Austin*)

CONSTRUCTION DOCUMENTATION

|||||||||||||||||||||||||||||||||||||||||||||||||||||||||||||||||||||||||||||||||||||||||||||||||||||||||||||||||||||||||||||||||||

The construction documentation (CD) phase is when you produce the legal construction documents that include the drawings and technical specification book. Both of these items must have an architect's stamp and signature prior to submittal to the city for building permits. Any consultants to the job will also add to the drawings and specification book using their respective licensing stamp.

The drawings are plans, elevations, sections, schedules, and details needed to build the project. The specifications are a bound book containing all the contract and noncontract documents for a construction project except the drawings and agreements. It outlines all the parties involved with the project and the technical information needed to supplement the drawings.

The CD phase includes the following deliverables:

- The following documents, stamped, dimensioned, noted, and properly cross-referenced
    - Floor, furniture, mechanical, plumbing, electrical, and lighting plans
    - Elevations, sections, and details
    - Window and door schedules
    - Room finish schedules with all materials and finishes
- Coordinated drawings from consultants and engineers
- Stamped specification book

Technical overall roof and site plan for the construction documents. (*Photograph courtesy of the Visual Resources Collection, School of Architecture, The University of Texas at Austin*)

These documents are submitted to all concerned parties, including to those in the city in which the job will be built. Changes to these documents, once submitted for review, are called addendums. They are numbered and cataloged to ensure that all parties get the proper information.

While the documents are being created, full-scale models of a construction method or a detail for specific areas of concern may be created to ensure the final building success. They are referred to in the industry as mock-ups. They can also take place during the next phase, the construction administration step, for specific finishes or coordination of finishes.

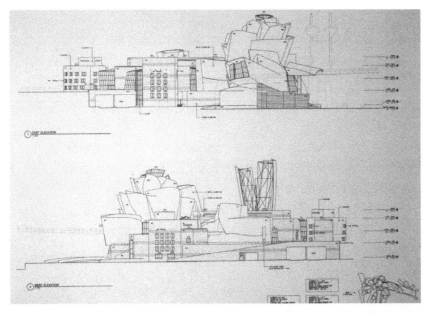

A sheet from the technical construction drawings that shows two exterior elevations of the building. (*Photograph courtesy of the Visual Resources Collection, School of Architecture, The University of Texas at Austin*)

A partial mock-up of a portion of the building skin. Mock-ups are made to ensure the product is up to the designer's standards and to confirm construction. (*Photograph courtesy of the Visual Resources Collection, School of Architecture, The University of Texas at Austin*)

CONSTRUCTION ADMINISTRATION

The construction administration (CA) phase of a project is during the actual building of the space or building. The main focus of this phase is to ensure that the project is being built to the level and specification that the design team desires upon completion.

Any changes to the documents in this phase are called change orders. Change orders may require additional materials and money. Like addendums they are numbered and cataloged.

Some tasks associated with CA should be done prior to the project being built.

- Submit the contract documents as the client's agent to the proper parties.
- Confirm that permits were obtained prior to the start of construction.

Other tasks are done while the project is being built:

- Review and approve shop drawings and material and finish samples, submittals (or mock-ups) to confirm that all the proper items and custom millwork are consistent with the submitted documents

  - Mock-ups, or submittals, in this phase are small installations that the contractor will oversee and the design team will approve before the entire space is built.

    - A 12 in. x 12 in. piece of drywall can be laid out by the tile subcontractor with all the different manufacturers' tiles and grout being used for a pattern on a restroom wall for example. This then demonstrates that the subcontractor has all the correct tile, sizes, colors, and grout in the proper locations prior to tiling an entire wall or project.

- Conduct site visits and field inspections of the project throughout construction to monitor the contractors' progress.

- Oversee the installation of FF&E.

Toward the end of the project, the CA representative should

- Prepare lists, called *punch lists,* of items that still need to be installed, repaired, and replaced by the contractor prior to the client's moving into the space.

- Prepare a punch list of any furniture issues that need to be corrected by the furniture installer.

Detail of metal framework on the exterior of the museum. (*Photograph courtesy of the Visual Resources Collection, School of Architecture, The University of Texas at Austin*)

An overall exterior view of the construction. (*Photograph courtesy of the Visual Resources Collection, School of Architecture, The University of Texas at Austin*)

Interior construction of a gallery space in the museum. (*Photograph courtesy of the Visual Resources Collection, School of Architecture, The University of Texas at Austin*)

Interior construction of a multi-story space in the museum. (*Photograph courtesy of the Visual Resources Collection, School of Architecture, The University of Texas at Austin*)

POSTOCCUPANCY EVALUATION

The final phase of the design process includes accessing how successful the project was for all of the parties involved. This is referred to as the postoccupancy evaluation (POE). At the very minimum, the design team should evaluate the internal success of the job.

Most firms will also ask the client for feedback on the usability of the design of the space as well as the working relationship with the firm.

STUDENT DOCUMENTATION

||||||||||||||||||||||||||||||||||||||||||||||||||||||||||||||||||||||||||||||||||||||||||||||||||||||||||||||||||||||||||||||||||||

Examples of student work will be seen through the first three steps of the design process of a restaurant. Although these drawings are done in the profession, very few are kept and documented publicly, as firms and clients keep them for their own design records.

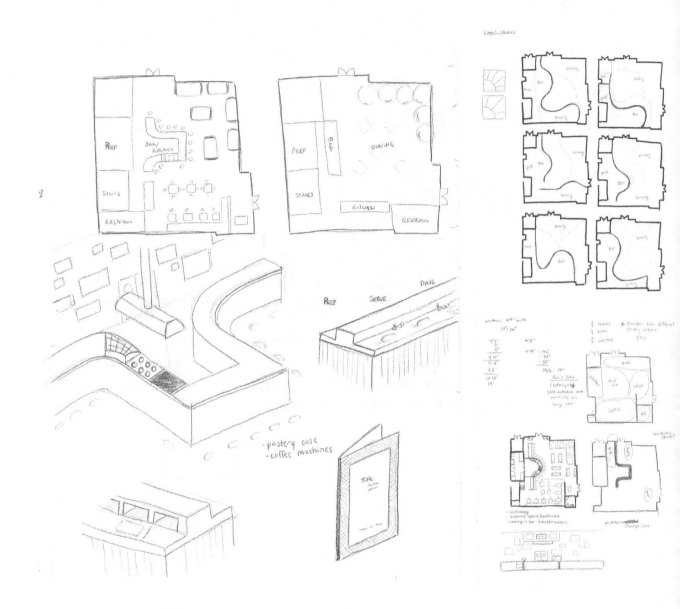

These pages represent a condensed demonstration of the programming and schematic design phases. The development of a floor plan from bubble diagrams and square footage analysis to a few furniture layouts as well as the early stages of design development including a three-dimensional study for the bar area.

(Illustrations by Megan Pfau)

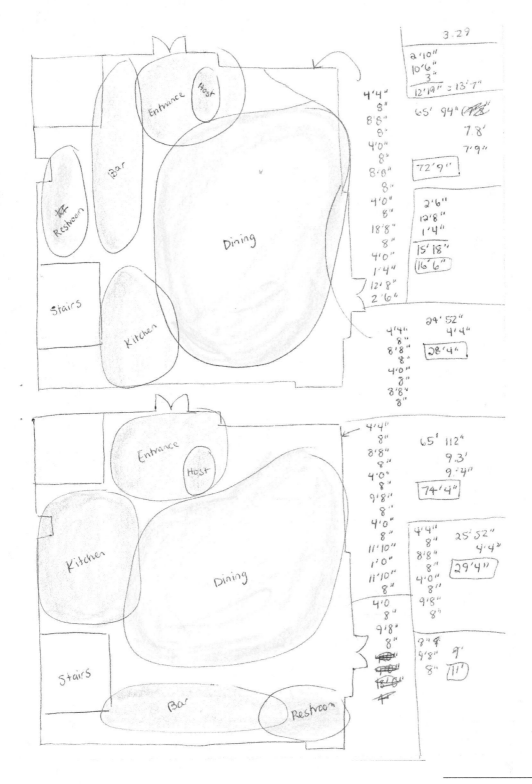

3.29

2'10"
10'6"
3"
12'19" = 13'7"

65' 94"
7.8'
7'9"

72'9"

4'4"
8"
8'8"
8"
4'0"
8"
8'8"
8"
4'0"
8"
18'8"
8"
4'0"
1'4"
12'8"
2'6"

2'6"
12'8"
1'4"
15'18"
16'6"

24' 52"
4'4"
28'4"

4'4"
8"
8'8"
8"
4'0"
8"
8'8"
8"

4'4"
8"
8'8"
8"
4'0"
8"
9'8"
8"
4'0"
8"
11'10"
1'0"
11'10"
8"
4'0
8"
9'8"
8"

65' 112"
9.3'
9'4"
74'4"

4'4"
8"
8'8"
8"
4'0"
8"
9'8"
8"

25' 52"
4'4"
29'4"

8'8"
9'8"
8"

9'
11'

The Design Process | 97

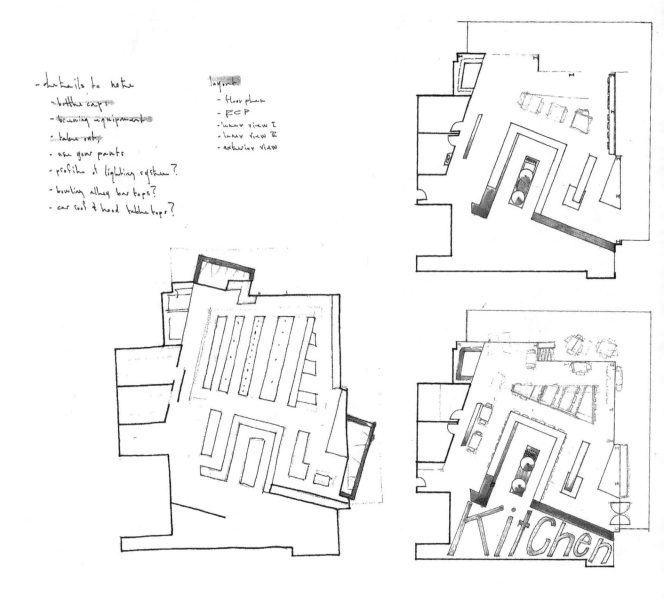

The schematic design of a restaurant is seen with a concept board and the development of the floor plan.
(*Illustrations by Sam Nitcher*)

CHROME HORSE BREWING
Chrome Horse Brewing
Chrome Horse Brewing

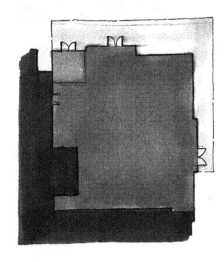

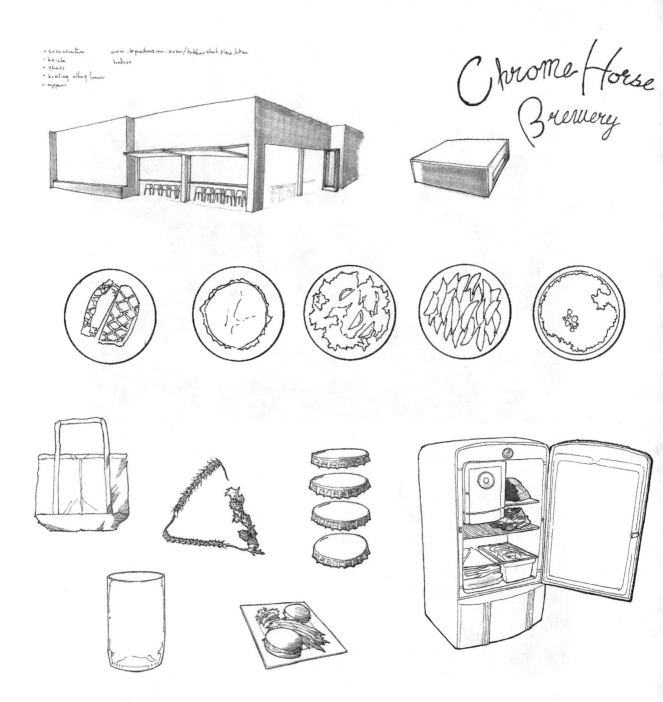

Documentation of the design development phase for the graphic identity and interior design of a restaurant.

(Illustrations by Sam Nitcher)

Perspective drawings done near the end of the design development phase are finished with color and graphic identity elements from earlier sketches. Pages 102–108 show the development from perspective drawings to the final renderings that will be mounted and presented to the client.

(Illustrations by Sam Nitcher)

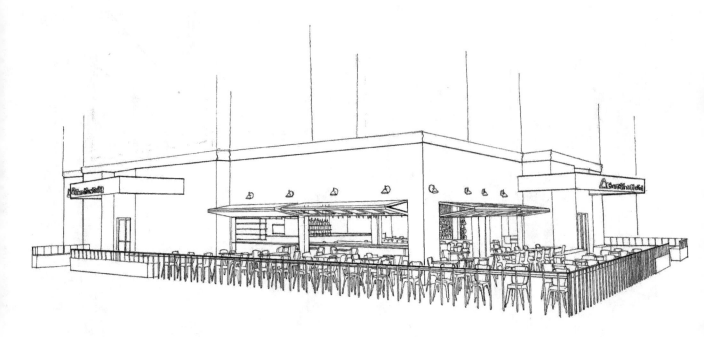

Chrome Horse Brewing

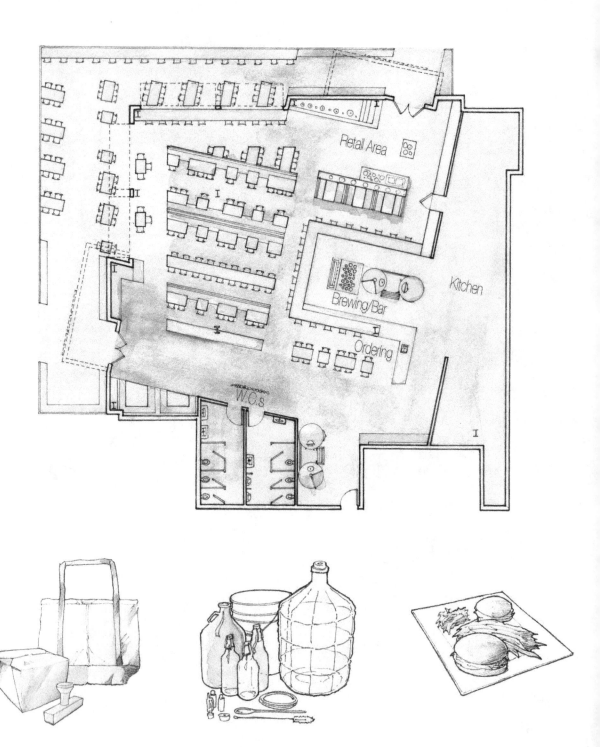

Retail Area

Kitchen

Brewing/Bar

Ordering

W.C.s

SUMMARY

||||||||||||||||||||||||||||||||||||||||||||||||||||||||||||||||||||||||||||||||||||||||||

The design process is sometimes long and hard to navigate, but relying on these steps ensures that it will be complete. While you are in school, keep every sketch, photograph every model, scan every inspiration, and document your design process. It will provide valuable insight into your abilities to design, and potential employers will want to see this type of work in your portfolio.

INDEX

||||||||||||||||||||||||||||||||||||||||||||||||||||||||||||||||||||||||||||||||||||||||||||

CPSIA information can be obtained
at www.ICGtesting.com
Printed in the USA